EARTHQUAKES

SEYMOUR SIMON

Smithsonian | **Collins**
An Imprint of HarperCollinsPublishers

To my grandnieces and grandnephews:
Bryan, Dena, Debbie, David, Alex, Michael, and Daniel

PHOTO AND ART CREDITS
p. 4, © Tom Wagner/Corbis SABA; p. 15, © Roger Ressmeyer/Corbis; p. 19, Fabrizio Bensch/Reuters/Corbis;
p. 21, © Benjamin Lowy/Corbis; pp. 30–31, © John K. Nakata/Terraphotographics/BPS; p. 32, © Richard Nairin/Photo
Researchers, Inc.; all other photographs courtesy of the National Geophysical Data Center/NOAA. Drawings on page 8 by Ann
Neumann; maps on pages 11 and 12 by Arlene Goldberg.
The name of the Smithsonian, Smithsonian Institution and the sunburst logo
are registered trademarks of the Smithsonian Institution.
Collins is an imprint of HarperCollins Publishers.

Earthquakes
Copyright © 1991 by Seymour Simon
Manufactured in China. All rights reserved.
No part of this book may be used or reproduced in any manner whatsoever without written permission except in the case of brief
quotations embodied in critical articles and reviews. For information address HarperCollins Children's Books, a division of
HarperCollins Publishers, 1350 Avenue of the Americas, New York, NY 10019.
www.harperchildrens.com
Library of Congress Cataloging-in-Publication Data
Simon, Seymour.
Earthquakes / Seymour Simon.
p. cm.
Summary: Examines the phenomenon of earthquakes, describing how and where they occur, how they can be predicted,
and how much damage they can inflict.
ISBN-10: 0-06-087714-6 (trade bdg.) — ISBN-13: 978-0-06-087714-9 (trade bdg.)
ISBN-10: 0-06-087715-4 (pbk.) — ISBN-13: 978-0-06-087715-6 (pbk.)
1. Earthquakes—Juvenile literature. [1. Earthquakes.] I. Title.
QE521.3.S54 1991   90-19328
551.2'2—dc20   CIP
                                                                                                       AC
1 2 3 4 5 6 7 8 9 10
❖
Revised Edition

Smithsonian Mission Statement

For more than 160 years, the Smithsonian has remained true to its mission, "the increase and diffusion of knowledge." Today the Smithsonian is not only the world's largest provider of museum experiences supported by authoritative scholarship in science, history, and the arts but also an international leader in scientific research and exploration. The Smithsonian offers the world a picture of America, and America a picture of the world.

Natural History Mission Statement

We inspire curiosity, discovery, and learning about nature and culture through outstanding research, collections, exhibitions, and education.

The earth beneath our feet usually feels solid and firm. Yet a million times each year—an average of once every thirty seconds—somewhere around the world the ground shakes and sways. We call this an earthquake.

Most earthquakes are too small to be noticed by people; only sensitive scientific instruments record their passage. But hundreds of earthquakes every year are strong enough to change the face of the land. A large earthquake in Kobe, Japan, in 1995, toppled this freeway onto its side and cracked the roadway in numerous places. This picture is an example of the enormous destruction an earthquake can cause in a heavily populated area.

On the morning of September 19, 1985, a major earthquake struck Mexico City. It killed ten thousand people and injured another twenty thousand. Hundreds of buildings were destroyed, including homes and stores, hotels and hospitals, and schools and businesses. This multilevel parking garage (center right) collapsed like a house of cards, while some of the neighboring buildings suffered only slight damage.

BLOCKS AT REST   STRESS BUILDS UP ALONG THE FAULT   THE ENERGY IS RELEASED

Most earthquakes take place in Earth's crust, a five- to thirty-mile-deep layer of rocks that covers our planet. Cracks in the rocks, called faults, run through the crust. In one type of fault, called a strike-slip fault, the rocks on one side of the fault try to move past the rocks on the other side, causing energy to build up. For years, friction will hold the rocks in place. But finally, like a stretched rubber band, the rocks suddenly snap past each other. The place where this happens is called the focus of an earthquake.

From the focus, the energy of the earthquake speeds outward through the surrounding rocks in all directions. The shocks may last for less than a second for a small earthquake to several minutes for a major one. Weaker shocks, called aftershocks, can follow an earthquake on and off for days or weeks.

Sections of the crust have slipped past each other along two strike-slip faults and offset this ridge in Wyoming (left). Sometimes one side of a fault will slip up over the other. This is what happened along this highway in the Mojave Desert of California (right). This kind of upward movement is called a thrust fault.

Four out of five of the world's earthquakes take place along the rim of the Pacific Ocean, a zone called the Pacific Ring of Fire. Alaska, Washington, Oregon, California, Mexico, the west coasts of Central and South America, and the east coasts of New Zealand, the Philippines, Japan, and Russia (Kamchatka and the Kuriles) are all located along the Pacific Ring of Fire. Another major earthquake zone stretches through Italy, Greece, Turkey, and Armenia to the Middle East and into Asia.

In the United States, almost half of the earthquakes each year occur in southern California. In other sections of the United States, earthquakes are rare.

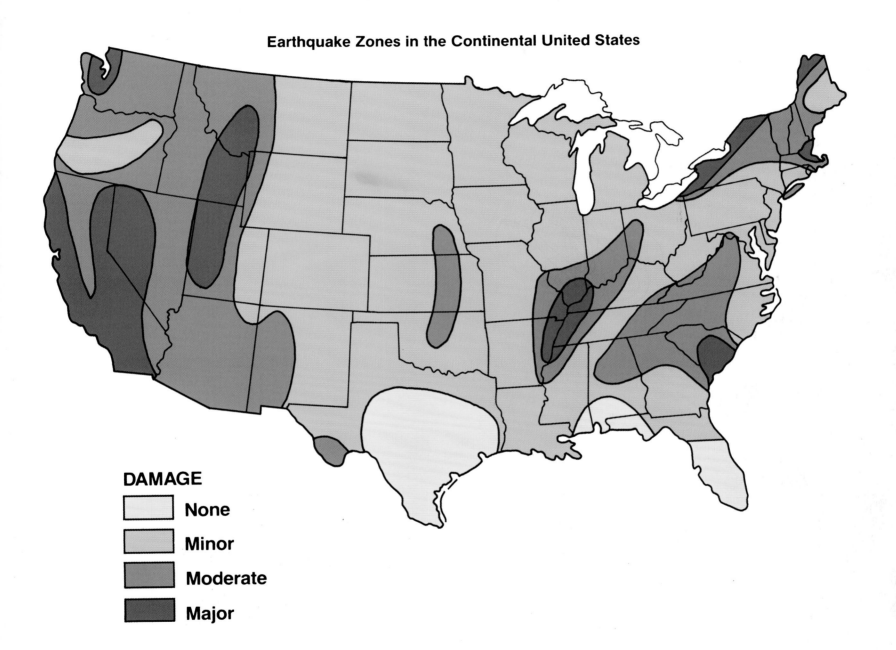

Earthquake Zones in the Continental United States

DAMAGE
None
Minor
Moderate
Major

Earthquakes Around the World

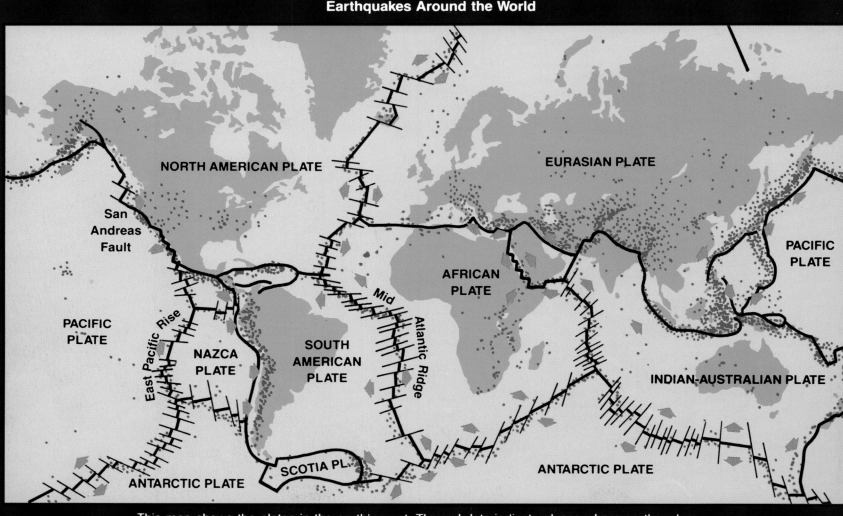

NORTH AMERICAN PLATE

EURASIAN PLATE

San Andreas Fault

PACIFIC PLATE

PACIFIC PLATE

AFRICAN PLATE

East Pacific Rise

NAZCA PLATE

SOUTH AMERICAN PLATE

Mid Atlantic Ridge

INDIAN-AUSTRALIAN PLATE

ANTARCTIC PLATE

SCOTIA PL.

ANTARCTIC PLATE

This map shows the plates in the earth's crust. The red dots indicate places where earthquakes have occurred.

Why do most earthquakes in the United States occur in California? The answer lies deep within Earth. Our planet's solid rocky crust floats on the mantle, a 1,800-mile-thick layer of very hot and dense rock that slowly churns around like a huge pot of boiling soup in very slow motion. The slowly moving mantle carries along the solid crust, which is cracked like an eggshell into a number of huge pieces called plates.

The plates float slowly about on the mantle up to four inches a year. As the plates move, they run into or pull away from each other, producing enormous strains in the rocks along their edges. The United States and Canada are riding on the North American plate, which is slowly moving against the Pacific plate. The colliding plates cause most of the earthquakes along the West Coast. But earthquakes can occur anywhere there are stresses in underlying rocks.

The San Andreas Fault is the boundary line between the North American and the Pacific plates. It winds seven hundred miles through southern California to just north of San Francisco, where it heads west across the floor of the Pacific Ocean. Along the way, it slashes under houses and dams, across deserts and farms, and through towns and cities where more than 20 million people live. Dozens of small- to medium-sized earthquakes occur along this fault each year. Scientists think that a huge, deadly earthquake will strike along the San Andreas Fault in the near future.

The 1906 San Francisco earthquake was one of the most violent earthquakes ever recorded. It was felt over an area of 375,000 square miles, more than twice the size of California. More than three thousand people lost their lives in the earthquake and the following fires. This view shows San Francisco in flames hours after the earthquake. The fires alone destroyed 28,000 buildings in the city.

This fence was broken and offset eight feet by the movement of the San Andreas Fault during the 1906 earthquake. Besides the widespread strike-slip (side-to-side) motion along the fault (above), there was also vertical movement of as much as three feet in some places.

How do you measure and compare the sizes of earthquakes? The size cannot be judged solely by the damage to buildings or the number of people killed. That's because a medium earthquake close to a large city will cause more destruction than will a larger earthquake in an unpopulated area.

Seismographs are the instruments that scientists use to measure earthquake shocks. Modern seismographs record their data to a computer and are able to detect a tiny earth tremor thousands of miles away. Seismologist Xiaohui Yuan of Germany's Geoscientific Research Institute points to the shockwaves that were recorded in blue in this digital graph (right) of the March 28, 2005, earthquake off the island of Sumatra.

There are hundreds of seismographic stations all over the world that time the arrival of earthquake waves. Scientists use the measurements to find an earthquake's timing, magnitude, and location (latitude, longitude, and depth).

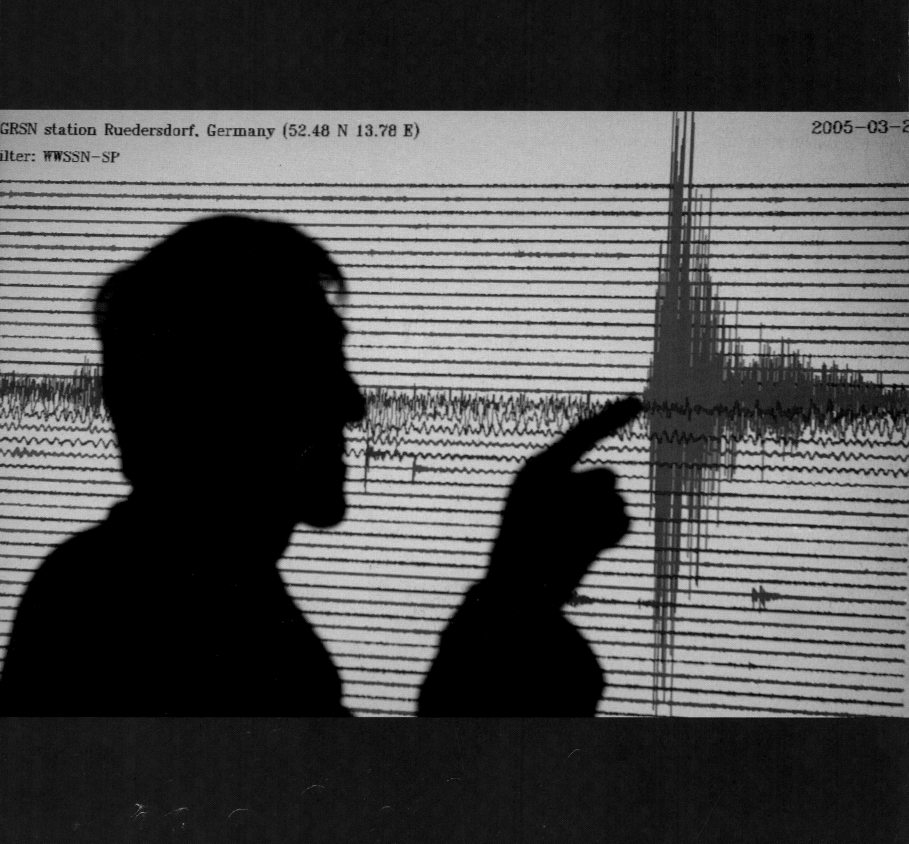

Scientists use the Richter Scale to measure an earthquake's magnitude, the amount of energy it releases. Each number on the Richter Scale stands for an earthquake that is ten times more powerful than the number below it. You would hardly notice a magnitude-2 earthquake, but a magnitude-3 earthquake is ten times greater and easily felt by everyone. The scale has no upper end, but any earthquake that registers 6 or more is considered a major earthquake.

The earthquake off the island of Sumatra on December 26, 2004, registered a 9.0 magnitude and caused huge earthquake-formed sea waves called tsunamis. The enormous earthquake and tsunami waves killed more than 200,000 people and caused immense destruction in several countries.

Scientists use observations as well as instruments to measure the effects of an earthquake. The Mercali Intensity Scale uses observations of the earthquake damage to rate it on a scale ranging from I, where the effects are scarcely noticeable, to XII, where damage is total and the ground heaves in waves. Usually, the intensity is greatest near the center of the earthquake and smaller farther away from the center. But other factors, such as the soil in the area and the construction of the buildings, are also important.

For example, the earthquake that shook the San Francisco area in October 1989 (during the World Series) measured 7.1 on the Richter Scale. On the Mercali scale, it measured X to XI in the Marina district (shown here), where the houses are built on loose soil, but only VI or VII in other parts of the city, where the houses suffered much less damage.

Sand, mud, and water sometimes bubble up during earthquakes, gushing water and soil like miniature mud volcanoes. These "sand boils" are particularly dangerous to buildings. In places where water is close to the surface, sandy layers turn into quicksand, and buildings tilt and crumble. During the 1989 San Francisco earthquake, sand boils erupted in basements and yards and beneath houses all over the Marina district.

These apartment houses in Niigata, Japan, tilted and tumbled as a result of an earthquake in 1964. The buildings tilted when the soil beneath the foundations turned to quicksand. About a third of the city sank by as much as six feet.

On the afternoon of Good Friday, March 27, 1964, Anchorage, Alaska, was shaken apart by the most violent earthquake ever recorded in the United States. It measured 8.4 on the Richter Scale. Government Hill Elementary School was split in two when the ground beneath it dropped. Houses began sliding apart, giant cracks opened in the pavement, and the ground rolled in huge waves. In the first three days after the earthquake, three hundred aftershocks shook the buildings that remained standing.

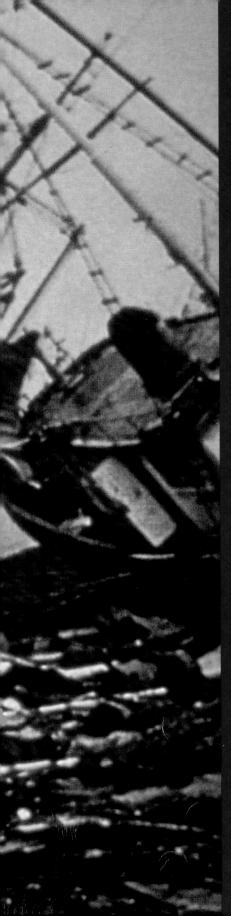

The Good Friday earthquake brought another type of destruction along the coastline. The focus of the earthquake was deep beneath the waters of Prince William Sound in the Gulf of Alaska. The earthquake acted like a giant paddle churning the waters.

Tsunamis battered the land for hours. An entire section of the waterfront at the port of Seward cracked off and slid into the ocean. Boats were overturned, buildings broke apart, and everything was left in a tangled mess.

The tsunamis moved across the Pacific at speeds of hundreds of miles an hour, reaching as far as Hawaii and even Japan, four thousand miles away.

Scientists have learned much about earthquakes and their effects. They can measure even the slightest movements along faults. But we need to know much more about earthquakes before we can predict weeks or even days in advance when a big one will hit. Until then, proper building design can help lessen their effects. We now know that houses in earthquake-prone areas should be built on solid rock and not on sand, for example. In California and Japan, new houses are designed to be earthquake-resistant.

It also helps to know what to do when an earthquake strikes. If you are indoors, get under a heavy table, desk, or bed. Stay away from windows, mirrors, or high cabinets. If you are in a high building, stay out of the elevators and stairways. If you are outdoors, move away from high buildings, walls, power poles, or any other tall objects. If possible, move to an open area. Above all, remain calm and don't worry. The chances of your being hurt in an earthquake are very, very slight.